Dear Blanca,
Wishing you a wonderful 2005!
Thank you for all of your efforts.
Karen Clausen

CONQUERING ADVERSITY

Six Strategies to Move You and Your Team Through Tough Times

CHRISTOPHER NOVAK

FOREWORD BY DAVID COTTRELL

Conquering Adversity

Six Strategies to Move
You and Your Team
Through Tough Times

Inquiries regarding permission for use of the material contained in this book should be addressed to:

CornerStone Leadership Institute
P.O. Box 764087
Dallas, TX 75376
888.789.LEAD

Printed in the United States of America
ISBN: 0-9746403-8-7

Credits

Editors
Alice Adams
Sue Coffman

Design, art direction, and production
Back Porch Creative, Plano, TX

For
Ryan, Jeannette and Connor

and
Cynthia and Hunter

*Never trade tomorrow's dreams
for yesterday's nightmares.*

Conquering Adversity:
Six Strategies to Move You and Your Team Through Tough Times

FOREWORD

Chris Novak understands adversity and what it takes to overcome it. He weathered the life-changing storm of losing his precious wife and unborn son and from that experience has created a guide that will benefit all of us.

This book needs to be read by everyone.

Adversity occurs without warning. It does not wait until we are ready, doesn't check our schedules and will not give us time to put a team in place or develop a contingency plan. Adversity is an insidious menace, disrespecting age, titles, achievements, wealth and tenure.

The sources of adversity are endless – life, health, family, work, finances, addiction, relationships – and each one challenges us to be more than we believe we could ever be.

When life is good, it is human nature to believe we are immune to the negatives others experience. We often settle into an "It will never happen to me" mind-set, a "not in my backyard" mentality.

Then, when adversity strikes, we are shocked, disbelieving, unprepared and often immobilized by the event, even though some mechanism of the human spirit keeps us moving forward, one foot after the other.

The unfortunate reality is that adversity is inevitable, often appearing to be a series of insurmountable challenges that invade our personal lives and threaten to derail our professional performance.

These are moments in our lives when we need someone

extraordinary to lead us. We need a hero. The good news is that there is help – an inner hero waiting to be discovered and unleashed at the very moment we need a champion most.

Conquering Adversity highlights *Six Strategies* to help us deal with tough times – **Affirmation, Expectation, Communication, Locomotion, Collaboration** and **Celebration** – strategies that have been tested in the fires of real-life crises and offer a proven plan to create successful personal and professional results amid the ashes of life's challenges. The principles in this book are absolutely foundational to your success in overcoming adversity.

Conquering Adversity is about:

♦ creating extraordinary success in the face of impossible odds.

♦ not trading tomorrow's dreams for yesterday's nightmares.

♦ delivering value at work by finding value at home.

Conquering Adversity is built on the premise that each one of us is bigger than any calamity, stronger than any problem, and that we have the power to move forward even in the most difficult circumstances. We CAN move mountains.

This book is inspiring. It introduces you to the hero you already are and gives you *Six Strategies* to discover that inner hero when it matters most.

When adversity comes, will you be ready?

Begin your journey now.

David Cottrell, President and CEO
CornerStone Leadership Institute

AUGUST 10TH

"This is the sheriff's department…Your wife has been in a bad accident…You need to go to the hospital immediately. Please…"

It was just another Monday when that call came in. As a human resources manager, I was meeting with two health insurance representatives at a ceramics manufacturer in Syracuse, New York. The phone rang, and I reached for it as I had done for the past seven years.

Nothing marked that moment as the beginning of something horrific, no hint that my world had already started to collapse, no warning that an inconceivable nightmare was unfolding. It was just a phone call.

As I picked up the receiver and glanced out my window at the overcast day with its gathering clouds, I could barely comprehend the words being spoken. It was just past 3:30 on the afternoon of

August 10th.

I do not remember hanging up the phone. I was shaking, my knees were weakening, my stomach was churning, and confusion held me in its grasp.

I ran to my boss, Plant Manager Wayne Zitkus, who was holding a manufacturing managers' meeting in a nearby conference room. I burst in, babbling something about having to get to the hospital because Cynthia had been in a bad accident.

Wayne stood up, reached into his pocket, pulled out his car keys and said, "I'll drive."

Racing through hospital corridors and up elevators, I found the trauma center and was stopped just short of double doors that read "RESTRICTED."

I kept asking, "Is she alive?" "Can I see her?" "How badly is she hurt?" "Is the baby all right?" Cynthia was seven months pregnant. The answers were few and incomplete. A nurse gently led me to a small room just outside the operating room.

For nearly two hours I waited. I sat. I paced. I cried. I prayed. Nurses came in and out to offer an encouraging word, but no one could give me news or peace. I could not talk or think. I could barely breathe.

Shortly after Wayne and I arrived at the hospital, my good friend Rick Synakowski ran down the hospital corridor to meet us. The news of Cynthia's crash was all over the media, and Rick had wasted no time in finding me.

In that small room, the three of us sat, waited and prayed. Three men at the edge of emotional strength kept a silent vigil that heaven would send a miracle. But there were to be no miracles that day.

He entered the tiny room shortly after 5 p.m., his surgeon's gown soaked in sweat, his hair matted and his face drawn, but the first thing I noticed was his eyes – looking away from me for just a fraction of a second.

When his eyes found mine again, I knew the truth. My tears started before he spoke a word.

In memory as in reality, that moment took on surreal dimensions. It was not happening, and yet I knew it was happening.

I was aware of the sounds and movements in the room, but it was as if I were watching it all from somewhere else.

The surgeon sat across from me, squeezing both my hands and fighting to hold his composure.

"Your wife died," he said. His voice was calm but broken. He told me how desperately they fought, how they did everything humanly possible. Yet, in spite of everything, my wife and baby had died on the operating table. He told me again how hard he had fought, how hard she had fought. He squeezed my hands tighter.

"I am so, so sorry. There was nothing we could do," the surgeon whispered. "I am so very, very sorry."

Then he hung his head and cried with us…for how long I don't know.

My tears were suddenly interrupted by an irrepressible desire to see her again.

"I have to see her," I said to the surgeon.

"I understand," he replied. "I'll take care of that right now."

In that moment of ultimate anguish, I needed to talk with her, just as I had always done. I needed to tell her that Ryan, our nine-year-old son, would grow up to be a man she would be proud of, that I would take care of him, that I would watch over him, love him, hold him, and raise him with every ounce of energy I had.

I told her that my love for her was eternal. I told her all these things, and I know she heard me. I know Cynthia heard me because the man that left her side had a new spirit in his broken heart, as if she had spoken, telling me to go and take care of our son.

I now had one more agonizing labor that day.

I did not know how to tell Ryan what had happened. How do you tell a little boy about such a terrible tragedy?

I just wanted this to be over, to awaken from what had to be a nightmare. Ryan was waiting for me as we pulled into Rick's driveway.

"What's wrong, Daddy?" he asked as I closed the truck door and took a deep breath. "What's wrong? Where's Mommy?"

His eyes looked up at me with such fear, such anxiety and such pain. Somehow, he had sensed the horror of the moment.

As a light rain started to soak both of us, I bent down, looked him in the eyes, put my arms out to his shoulders, and said the only words my mouth would form. "Ryan, I am so very sorry…"

His tears started.

"I don't know how to say this…"

Tears streamed down his cheeks, and I could feel him shaking.

As I went to hug him, Ryan bolted from my arms. Crying, angry and afraid, he shouted, "No, no, no…," and then he did the only thing a nine-year-old would know how to do when he was scared. He ran... from me, his pain and the horrible truth just handed to him. I ran after him, but realizing I could not catch him, I stopped.

"Ryan, I need you," I shouted through the rain. "I need you."

He stopped in his tracks, turned toward me and raced back to my open arms. I hugged him tightly, and we both just cried.

I did not need the lessons of 9-11 to remind me about the importance of family. I know firsthand what it is to have everything taken from you in the blink of an eye. I have lived the nightmare of answering a call that changes your life forever. I know what it is to pray for a miracle that never comes.

I know what it is to collapse in grief and cry so hard that your body convulses. I know what it is to lie awake night after night because it hurts too much to dream.

I also know how to stand back up. I live the Japanese proverb, "Knocked down seven times, stand up eight." I know what it takes to regain a life lost.

In the years since Cynthia and Hunter's death, I have discovered a strength, resilience and ability to move forward that I did not know I had. I found purpose, happiness and love amid the ashes of a shattered life. I have shared these insights with my son, with my family, with my friends and colleagues, and I have watched as these insights have helped all of us arrive at a place of peace and success in our personal and professional lives.

In time, I translated my experience into a motivational message that many people tell me has changed them for the better. *Conquering Adversity: Six Strategies to Move You and Your Team Through Tough Times* is the organized collection of insights, experiences and actions that made a difference in my life. They can make a difference in yours.

This book offers insights as unique as each individual. As you read it, consider the obstacles, barriers and adversities in your own life – at work and home. My story may be unique, but my message is universal, and for those who hear with their hearts, the outcome is always the same – a renaissance of inner strength that we all have.

Listen closely and feel the power.

STRATEGY # 1

AFFIRMATION

---

*The least of things with a meaning is worth more
in life than the greatest of things without it.*

~ Source Unknown ~

Steps in the **Affirmation** Strategy:

1. Identify bedrock values.

2. Acknowledge what is and is not lost.

3. Accept a healthy "selfishness."

The first of the Six Strategies – **Affirmation** – shows us where
to look first for our inner strength. Self-reflection and self-validation
give perspective on what we have to work with as we prepare to
engage crisis.

Affirmation acknowledges that YOU are one thing – sometimes
the only thing – that you can influence in the struggle to overcome
adversity, so know what you have to begin the journey.

Affirmation is personal validation, a search for individual clarity amid an otherwise obscured and emotional landscape. Adversity heightens our confusion, anxiety, anger and fear. We become unsure of ourselves, untrusting of our surroundings, even defeatist in our attitudes.

Adversity's onset is rapid and natural, but destructive as well. **Affirmation** breaks this decline and sharpens our vision, restoring a measure of confidence to help us make critical decisions.

Affirmation does not wish. **Affirmation** believes.

> Affirmation
> does not wish.
> **Affirmation**
> **believes.**

Wishing has no basis for its desired outcome, but believing is rooted in the understanding of self and purpose.

It is important to look deep inside our thoughts, feelings and dreams and to give voice to those silent engines that drive our actions, decisions and lives.

Most of us spend more time each week deciding what food to put into our carts at the grocery store than we spend understanding what values we put into our lives. **Affirmation** addresses this inequity.

STEP ONE

To take the first step with **Affirmation**, identify your bedrock values. In moments of extreme challenge, look inward and ask the important "what" questions. What truth do I believe? What certainties can I identify? What am I committed to achieving? What have I already overcome? What unshakable principles guide my actions? What are my core values?

These are not trivial questions, and they are best answered in the calm before a crisis. Looking for answers to **Affirmation** in the height of crisis is like chasing leaves in a windstorm. There's no time to focus and to gather the strength you need to move ahead.

What are bedrock values? They take many forms – love of family, a sense of faith, commitment to a cause, supreme optimism, a persistent spirit, a belief in doing what is right, an obligation to honor the truth, a realization that failure is not an option.

You may have found your bedrock values through previous challenges or hard lessons from past mistakes. They may have emerged as insights from trusted counsel, or faith in a higher purpose, or in the knowledge that you will not be defined by the problem but rather by how you act on that problem.

The answers to questions about your bedrock values come from your heart, not your head, so let passion trump reason when examining core convictions.

Remember, heroes not only stand for something; they stand ON something – the unchanging certainty of deeply held beliefs – and that is where you find a solid footing to face every challenge.

In my experience, bedrock values started with the knowledge that being a father to Ryan was an unshakable commitment to Cynthia's memory. In that private moment at the hospital I spent with Cynthia, I promised to pour every ounce of whatever time I had left on this planet into raising Ryan into a healthy, happy, successful man. I would be there for him as long as he needed me.

Ryan had lost his mother, but I was determined he would not

lose a father to the same tragedy, starting with the premise that I could not fail him, would not fail him. From that, I realized that neither would I fail myself. I had never known what it was to quit on anything, and now was not the time to start.

Acknowledging that inner resilience, that inner strength – even when I could not see it – provided enough stability for me to regain a measure of self-confidence.

That's what bedrock values do for you: they give evidence of your capacity to cope, your potential to prevail. Bedrock values help you believe in yourself.

Writing a personal mission statement is one of the most powerful ways to practice **Affirmation**. In the same way that an organizational mission statement fuses purpose and passion, a personal mission statement boils down critical values, direction and motivation in your life.

The task of putting this all on paper requires you to reflect, evaluate and sharpen your vision. Make time after you finish this book to write a personal mission statement.

Identifying bedrock values at work brings the same sense of self-confidence that it brings to your personal life. Ask important "what" questions about your professional life.

These questions could begin with the following:

(1) What does my organization believe in?

(2) What does it stand for?

(3) What do I communicate in my work that contributes to our collective values?

(4) What have we already achieved as a team?

(5) What do we have the capacity to achieve?

Finding and sharing the answers to these questions are the foundation for building an organization of owners, not renters.

When people understand their personal and organizational value-driven character, purpose and passions, they tend to treat their places of employment with the care and respect of owners rather than the indifference and apathy of renters. They own their jobs and the work that they produce, and that is the first step in elevating a group of employees to a team of heroes.

Bedrock values also are the mortar that holds business ethics together – ethics all too frequently absent in today's workplace.

To thrive, organizations need leaders, teams and associates with strong, visible values. Imagine a workplace where values are as talked about as profits. How professionally and personally satisfying would it be to attend a meeting where the first item on the agenda was to discuss the impact of personal values on business success? Values that are visible are viable.

Values that are **visible** are **viable**.

Leaders set the tone for identifying bedrock values in simple but powerful ways. Establish a developmental goal for everyone on the team to complete a personal mission statement, give them a copy of this book, create a "Values Wall" at work, and invite people to post quotes, articles and ideas on how values contribute to better organizations and employees.

The applications of **Affirmation** in the workplace are endless.

Just remember – the time to discover values is before you need to rely on them.

STEP TWO

The second aspect of Affirmation is to recognize what is lost and what is not lost. It is natural in times of extreme duress to believe that everything is lost. Indeed, the greater the loss, the deeper the sense of hopelessness.

Despair is a quagmire that slows our ability to act and react by paralyzing our reasoning with fear of change – especially sudden, extreme change.

Fear is the power that adversity holds over us, and the more we dwell on our fear, the more power we give it. To escape fear's grip is to focus on what remains in place and is not lost rather than on what has changed or been lost.

Focusing on what is not lost helps us take a mental inventory of our situation. It is like the shipwrecked sailor gathering items that have washed ashore after the storm to see what may be of value and what is left to use. Lamenting what is not there adds nothing to the sailor's ability to survive. The focus must be on how to creatively use whatever can be salvaged.

In essence, **Affirmation** teaches us to become emotional archeologists, searching the ruins of our situation for remnants of what is still valuable, relevant and important. By concentrating on the positive aspects of our situation – rather than dwelling on the negative ones – we create a sense of optimism and energy that help us go forward through a crisis and to make the most of limited resources in challenging times.

In my own experience, the magnitude of the change I suddenly experienced was crushing. In the span of a few hours, I went from a confident human resources executive with a beautiful wife, a wonderful nine-year-old son, and a

> By concentrating on the **positive**... we create a sense of **optimism** and **energy**.

second son less than two months away to a grieving single parent whose world had been devastated. Change? This was not change. It was the obliteration of almost everything I knew.

Standing among the pieces of my shattered life, I found it difficult to see anything other than senseless destruction. It was easy to see what had been lost. It took a different kind of strength, a higher level of strength, to see what had not been lost.

Using this newly discovered inner strength helped me first realize that everything had not been lost – starting with Ryan and me. We were still here. Ryan needed a father more than ever, and I needed to be a father more than ever. We had not lost that bond.

My family, my friends, my colleagues and my neighbors had not been lost, and they were there to help. My confidence had been shattered when I lost my soul mate, but my persistent nature had not been lost, and I was determined not to fail her. I had also not lost the love that Cynthia and I shared for nearly twenty years... since the time we met as seniors in high school...and those memories could never be taken away. They were Cynthia's gift to me for the rest of my life.

By focusing on what had not been lost in this tragedy, I freed my mind to look past the paralysis of the moment and work on the critical next steps. My grief did not diminish, but I was able to function in that grief because I understood that very important treasures remained.

In our workplace, we rarely encounter so violent or dramatic a change. Yet change still challenges our organizations and creates adversities for the people impacted by the change.

> **Learning** to evaluate the **impact of change**... brings a more productive **perspective**.

Managing change effectively is one of the top priorities for most companies because it is not something we do well. Learning to evaluate the impact of change – based on what is not lost or constant as opposed to what has been lost and what differences we will encounter – brings a more productive perspective.

We know change is coming... that change is the only corporate constant. To cling to the status quo in today's business environment means to fall behind. However, with change come fear and adversity.

Changes in the people we work with, the customers we serve, the products we market, the procedures we follow, the team we're on, our supervisor, our staff, a senior executive or any host of new challenges create fear and anxiety. In these situations, the most productive approach is to spend energy discovering what has not changed and what resources are still available.

You can start with yourself – you're still able to bring your talents and energy to the moment. Help others see that despite the changes, there are things of value still intact and a potential for even greater success. Be a positive voice for keeping the focus on the work still to do and the resources that are still available.

STEP THREE

The final aspect of Affirmation is to practice a "healthy selfishness."

Sounds strange, right?

My experience has been that taking care of yourself, even amid adversity, is crucial to effective decision-making. A healthy selfishness includes keeping your physical well-being intact with sleep, proper nutrition and exercise. You cannot overcome extreme challenges when your physical health is deteriorating. The pressures of the moment will tempt you to set aside your own care, but resist that urge. Make time for yourself!

"Healthy selfishness" also means clinging to your bedrock values, even when it is not convenient. As you move forward through adversity, keeping even small commitments takes on disproportionate significance. However, this kind of selfishness is a matter of self-validation, of reinforcing a notion of some normalcy and control in a situation that can easily feel like a runaway train.

For example, one commitment I made was to read to Ryan every night before he went to bed. It became a ritual for us, one that I looked forward to with almost as much excitement as he did. Each night, we read one chapter from what we called "chapter books," a fiction series that held our interest and built anticipation for the next night's reading. The *Star Wars Young Jedi* series was our favorite, and we quickly developed the habit of checking bookstores for the latest release.

It did not matter what we had done that day or who objected to the late hour if we were past bedtime. I was determined to read with Ryan each night, if only a few pages. Most nights, we read some and talked some, but for years after his mother's death, we read chapter books every night.

For me, that experience reinforced the value of being a dad, of being needed each night for this special event. It wasn't that I was reading a book to Ryan. He was capable of doing that himself. More important, I was bonding with my son. I was hugging the little boy who needed to know he was not alone in the world. I was adding stability to our shaken reality. I was making myself available every night to catch some of his pain as it overflowed into our conversation. I was not just reading a book to Ryan. I was living one of my bedrock values. A healthy selfishness kept us moving forward.

As leaders, team members or associates, we can practice healthy selfishness by keeping even small commitments. Do we call someone back when we say we will? Are we prompt in keeping our appointments or arriving at meetings? If we promise someone an answer or information, does that person hear from us? If we commit to cover a shift for a colleague, do we keep that commitment?

It is the sum of kept promises, even small ones, that builds our credibility and effectiveness with colleagues. When we say we are going to do something, we follow through. It may be inconvenient.

It may be difficult. It may not be something we want to do, but if we commit to do something, it is a mark of our professionalism, even our integrity, to honor our commitments.

STRATEGY

1. **Identify bedrock values.**
2. **Acknowledge what is and is not lost.**
3. **Accept a "healthy selfishness."**

AFFIRMATION

At the conclusion of each of the *Conquering Adversity* chapters are **Insight Activities** that reinforce the learning points of the *Strategy* in that chapter. These **Insight Activities** can be completed as you read the book or after you have finished the entire book, but you are encouraged to make these activities a part of the *Conquering Adversity* experience.

Insight *Activity* ────────────────

♦ Complete the "Top 20" worksheet on the following page.
♦ Reflect on your choices.
♦ It will be difficult to choose between values that feel equally important, but the exercise of assigning them a ranking will help you internalize what you truly believe. Think about your choices.

Conquering Adversity

What Do We Value?
Your "Top 20"

Rank order the Values listed below from 1 (most valued) to 20 (least valued).

_____ Good Health

_____ Spiritual Fulfillment

_____ Free Time and Fun

_____ Financial Security

_____ Travel, Discovery, Adventure

_____ Learning and Teaching

_____ Peace of Mind

_____ Recognition

_____ Strong Work Ethic

_____ Respect of Others

_____ Love

_____ Friendships

_____ Professional Success

_____ Stability

_____ Close Family Relationships

_____ Creativity

_____ Service to Others

_____ Personal Integrity

_____ Persistence

_____ Optimism

STRATEGY

EXPECTATION

---

*"We must accept finite disappointment,
but never lose infinite hope."*

~ Martin Luther King, Jr ~

Steps in the **Expectation** Strategy:
1. Recognize that life is not fair,
   so don't expect it to be.
2. Apply optimism.
3. Avoid the "why?" traps.

Affirmation is our inner compass. **Expectation** is our direction.

Expectation establishes a mind-set that accepts what is and projects what can be. It is more than making lemonade from lemons — it is having no lemons and still visualizing a thriving lemonade business.

Adversity attacks our vision, limits our sight and blinds us with the challenges of the moment. **Expectation** refocuses the vision and takes us beyond today with a forward-thinking perspective. It does not ignore today's reality but it does not become mired in it, either.

Step One

The first step of the **Expectation** strategy is simple: "**Life is not fair, so don't expect it to be.**" Webster uses words like *just, equitable* and *dispassionate* as synonyms for *fair* – none of which reflects the reality of what happens when tragedy strikes.

There is nothing fair about a 37-year-old woman who is seven months pregnant dying after colliding with a reckless, drug impaired driver who is able to walk away from the crash. There is nothing fair about a nine-year-old boy having to live the rest of his life without the mother he loved so much. There is nothing fair about anything associated with that scenario, just as there is nothing fair about the woman who is diagnosed with breast cancer, the fireman who dies rescuing a family from arson, or the child who dies at the hands of an abusive adult.

The plain truth is that life is not fair, and we cannot expect it to be. Bad things happen to good people, and there is no universal law guaranteeing justice.

Somewhere in our maturation process we have to come to grips with these disturbing truths.

Work is not fair, either. No matter how well-intentioned or principled our organization, there is no escaping the fact that unfair things sometimes happen. We know that. We have experienced lack of fairness ourselves – sometimes more than we want to admit.

In some cases, we become the beneficiary of the injustice. At other times we are the injured party.

Good people make bad decisions – not because they're malicious but because they're human. Good leaders make mistakes – not intentionally, but they make mistakes nonetheless.

Do we accept this reality and measure persons or organizations on the totality of their efforts? Do we give management the benefit of the doubt when we disagree with decisions? Do we acknowledge that not everyone will see our actions as justified or consistent?

We should. We need to. We would want our colleagues to do the same for us.

The most important workplace translation of this insight is that we cannot allow ourselves to be held hostage to the inadvertent but inevitable injustices we will encounter. As leaders, team members or individual contributors, we must adjust our **Expectations** to accept the truth that life – and work – are not always fair and that even in this reality, we must excel.

We must never let even valid disappointment affect our performance, our attitude or our results.

STEP TWO

The second step in the **Expectation** strategy is to apply optimism.

We must expect to succeed. We must visualize ourselves conquering adversity. **Expectation** is about "seeing" our inner strength take over long before we find ourselves hanging over a precipice.

Another word for "**Expectation**

> We must **expect** to **succeed.**

without optimism" is desperation – and you won't find your hero in that morass, either.

Optimism takes some of the sting out of adversity. It helps us see things as they could be or should be rather than as they are. It reassures us that tomorrow can be better than today if we make it so.

I learned this lesson early in my experience with adversity:

> *It was the first morning after Cynthia died. I had spent the night in Ryan's room, barely closing my eyes for more than a few minutes and hugging my son through the countless sobs that came in his sleep.*
>
> *The sun was just coming up when I heard the radio click on in the master bedroom across the hall. Not wanting the music to awaken Ryan, I slid off the covers and walked into our bedroom to a gentle shock. The song on the radio at that instant was Shania Twain's "You're Still the One," – our song – the one Cynthia had dedicated to me on our fourteenth wedding anniversary less than two months before.*
>
> *"Our song" was the first thing I heard that morning, and I pictured us swaying to its reaffirming message of love in the living room while Ryan giggled at his parents' dancing.*
>
> *On that first terrible morning after the crash, I listened to the entire song and heard a bigger message. It helped me understand that I was not going to leave this home, not going to run from the memories, not going to retreat. I knew Ryan and I could be happy here again…that Cynthia wanted us to be happy again…that, for now, this was where we needed to be. My optimism was rooted in the fading melody of a familiar song and the strengthening image of memories not yet made.*

Leaders can underestimate the power of optimism in motivating their teams.

Research shows that optimistic salespeople outsell their competition by 37 percent and that a student's level of optimism is a better predictor of a college freshman's performance than SAT scores. Optimists live, on average, two years longer than pessimists, and the body's ability to fight diseases – such as cancer and AIDS – is unmistakably linked to a patient's level of positive thinking.

Optimism is a crucial choice we make in establishing **Expectations** for ourselves and others as we begin to move forward through adversity.

Psychologist Martin Seligman, in his book *Learned Optimism*, confirmed that optimists – even when their outlook is unfounded – accomplish more than so-called realists. In fact, the more difficult the task to be undertaken and the more pressure to succeed, the more important optimism becomes to the endeavor's success.

> **Optimism** is a crucial **choice** we make in establishing **expectations** for ourselves and others.

Secretary of State Colin Powell echoed that finding in his own words: "Spare me the grim litany of the 'realist.' Give me the unrealistic aspirations of the optimist any day."

Our workplaces are filled with the "grim litany of the realist." It is easy to criticize and then mask that negativism as realistic analysis. The unchallenged fact is that we need more optimism on the job. We need people who think like winners, talk like winners and act like winners.

Our organizations will thrive when our people can "see" tomorrow as better than today because they are making it better. Organizations need leaders who use the language of **Expectation**. Leaders who set a positive tone, praise progress and do not waste their efforts assigning blame when they can be assigning solutions will find team members eager to tackle the toughest challenges.

In the words of an optimist, mistakes become experience, letdowns become learning, crisis becomes challenge, and adversity becomes opportunity.

STEP THREE

The third step of the Expectation strategy is to avoid the "why?" traps.

As a natural extension of the first two elements, this third aspect of **Expectation** reminds us that searching for an answer to why something happened or why it happened to you or someone you care about is an exercise in futility. Concentrate instead on how you move forward.

My own experience offers insight into the paralysis of the "why?" trap and the liberation of avoiding its temptation:

> *Why did this happen?*
> *That question paralyzed my mind as I struggled deep into the night.*
> *Exhausted, shattered and frustrated with myself, I finally understood the answer. The truth was that there was no answer. No one could ever explain why this had happened.*

No reason could be found for why it was her car in that intersection at that moment. There were no answers, and there never would be.

But it was not answers I needed. It was peace with the question. It was not a rationale for what had happened but an acceptance of it.

The transition from seeking answers to "why?" to seeking peace and acceptance brought me to a point where I could see what really mattered...love.

I had to remind myself not to waste my time, emotions and energies searching for answers that are not there but to focus instead on moving forward.

How many "why?" traps do we encounter in our professional lives? How many times do we waste energy searching for why something happened instead of working on the next action needed for success? Why was she hired? Why did our schedule change? Why I was not promoted? Why didn't we get that customer? Why wasn't my raise as big as someone else's?

The possible "why?" traps are endless, and each one can be just as paralyzing as my own painful lesson. Spending time and energy searching for answers means we are stagnant, idle and unproductive.

Get past it. Move forward. The answer is not in what is behind you, but in what is ahead. It's not about why. It's about how – how I go forward. How do I earn the promotion next time? How do I make the new schedule work for our team? How can

> The **answer** is not in what is behind **you**, but in what is **ahead.**

I win back that customer or find a new one? How can I earn a bigger raise next time?

Yesterday's issues are history, so leave them there. "Why?" traps lure us into a rearview mirror syndrome. It is impossible to drive a car by looking into the rearview mirror to see where we have been. Our priority is to see where we are going. In the same way, tackling adversity means moving forward with the knowledge that some questions need action, not answers.

Expectation makes us accountable – not for what has happened but for how we react. It sets standards for personal accountability and demands just a fraction more from us each day.

STRATEGY #

1. Realize that life is not fair, so don't expect it to be.

2. Apply optimism.

3. Avoid the "why?" traps.

EXPECTATION

Insight *Activity*

There is power in visualizing success.

Great athletes, artists, musicians and speakers testify to the connection between focused reflection and extraordinary performance. It programs us to win, and it is a powerful, positive habit.

Commit to a daily drill by setting aside just five minutes each day to quietly visualize where your life is going. This is quiet time to read your Personal Mission Statement, reflect on your values and "see" your future as you want it to be.

Winners "see" their success before they ever move toward it. Take time to visualize your direction.

STRATEGY # 3
COMMUNICATION

---

*"Do not save your loving speeches for your friends
till they are dead. Do not write them on their tombstones,
speak them rather now instead."*

~ Anna Cummins ~

Steps in the **Communication** Strategy:

1. Communicate with your heart.

2. Communicate now!

3. Invite others to help.

*Twenty-four hours before the tragedy, Cynthia had never
looked quite so beautiful. Smiling gently, with a warm
August sun radiating through her blonde hair, Cynthia had
the glow they say all pregnant women achieve – only she
had more. I looked at her sitting there, tummy bulging from
seven months of carrying our miracle baby – Hunter James –
and I knew our world was right.*

We had tried for eight years to have a second child, and only when we accepted the single blessing of our nine-year-old son did Providence smile on us with another. Cynthia was beautiful – so content, so happy, so filled with love and life.

She must have sensed my admiration because she tipped her head slightly, glanced down and then looked back up into my eyes and smiled. In that moment, we smiled at each other in a way that husbands and wives sometimes forget to as the years go by, smiled as we did when we were high school sweethearts.

Now, twenty years later, she still had that look, the one that reminded me I had fallen in love with my best friend and soul mate. In that moment, she found words that echo in my mind every day: "Honey, if we never have any more than we have right now, we have everything we ever wanted."

How important are her words to me now? How much does it mean to me to know she was supremely happy and content with the life we had built together? What impact did that one sentence have on the rest of my life?

The answers are immediate and profound.

STEP ONE

Communicate with your heart. By sharing her heart, Cynthia helped me find peace with what would follow. By not assuming that I knew these feelings, she painted an indelible image in my mind of how much she loved me, our family and our life – right up to the last day of her life. The power of emotion is in its

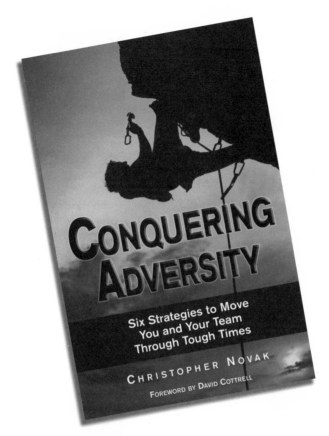

CONQUERING ADVERSITY

Six Strategies to Move You and Your Team Through Tough Times

CHRISTOPHER NOVAK

FOREWORD BY DAVID COTTRELL

3 Easy Ways to Order Copies for Your Management Team!

1. Complete the order form on back and fax to 972-274-2884

2. Visit www.cornerstoneleadership.com

3. Call 1-888-789-LEAD (5323)

CornerStone
Leadership Institute

The Ant and the Elephant is a different kind of book for a different kind of leader! A great story that teaches that we must lead ourselves before we can expect to be an effective leader of others. **$12.95**

Start Right – Stay Right is every employee's straight-talk guide to personal responsibility and job success. Perfect for every employee at every level, from seasoned co-workers to new staff additions. **$9.95**

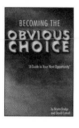

Too Many Emails contains dozens of tips and techniques to increase your email effectiveness and efficiency. **$9.95**

175 Ways to Get More Done in Less Time has 175 really, really good suggestions that will help you get things done faster... and usually better. **$9.95**

Becoming the Obvious Choice is a roadmap showing each employee how they can maintain their motivation, develop their hidden talents, and become the best. **$9.95**

Leadership ER is a powerful story that shares valuable insights on how to achieve and maintain personal health, business health and the critical balance between the two. Read it and develop your own prescription for personal and professional health and vitality. **$14.95**

Goal Setting for Results addresses the fundamentals of setting and achieving your goal of moving yourself and your organization from where you are, to where you want (and need) to be! **$9.95**

136 Effective Presentation Tips provides you with inside tips from two of the best presenters in the world. **$9.95**

You Gotta Get In The Game...Playing to Win in Business, Sports and Life provides direction on how to get into and win the game of life and business. **$14.95**

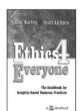

Ethics 4 Everyone is a real-world guide for corporate leaders on how to lead with integrity. Following these guidelines will help your company win the right way. **$9.95**

Personal Development Package

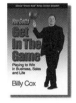

$119.95

☑ YES! Please send me extra copies of *Conquering Adversity*!
1-30 copies $14.95   31-100 copies $13.95   100+ copies $12.9

Conquering Adversity	____ copies X _____	= $ __

Additional Personal Development Resources

The Ant and the Elephant	___ copies X $12.95	= $ —
Start Right – Stay Right	___ copies X $19.95	= $ —
Too Many Emails	___ copies X $9.95	= $ —
175 Ways to Get More Done in Less Time	___ copies X $9.95	= $ —
Becoming the Obvious Choice	___ copies X $9.95	= $ —
Leadership ER	___ copies X $14.95	= $ —
Goal Setting for Results	___ copies X $9.95	= $ __
136 Effective Presentation Tips	___ copies X $9.95	= $ __
You Gotta Get in the Game	___ copies X $14.95	= $ __
Ethics 4 Everyone	___ copies X $9.95	= $ __
Personal Development Package (includes all 11 books listed above)	___ packs X $119.95	= $ __
	Shipping & Handling	$ __
	Subtotal	$ __
	Sales Tax (8.25%-TX Only)	$ __
	Total (U.S. Dollars Only)	$ __

Shipping and Handling Charges

Total $ Amount	Up to $50	$51-$100	$101-$249	$250-$1199	$1200-$2999	$3
Charge	$6	$9	$16	$30	$80	$

Name _____ Job Title _____

Organization _____ Phone _____

Shipping Address _____ Fax _____

Billing Address _____ Email _____

City _____ State _____ Zip _____

❏ Please invoice (Orders over $200) Purchase Order Number (if applicable) _____

Charge Your Order: ❏ MasterCard   ❏ Visa   ❏ American Express

Credit Card Number _____ Exp. Date _____

Signature _____

❏ Check Enclosed (Payable to CornerStone Leadership)

expression. The power of true **Communication** is learning to speak our hearts with the same ease that we speak our minds.

Communication is the third *Strategy* because it conveys both **Expectation** and **Affirmation**.

It is about projecting what we feel, what we know, what we believe. It gives voice to those values, dreams and inspirations that we have affirmed and articulates the **Expectations** we have established. **Communication** rails against the silence of assumption.

Communication is not about talking. It's about sharing.

People talk constantly but rarely communicate. The act of merely talking moves words, facts and figures in order to receive something. Communicating, on the other hand, shares feelings, emotions and trust in order to give something.

Communication
is not about talking.
It's about **sharing**.

Communication removes misconceptions, assumptions and doubts and refreshes the bond between people.

It is difficult for some individuals to become comfortable expressing their feelings. It is easier to say what we think than share what we feel. Why? Because we don't practice the art of **Communication**. It's embarrassing. It's awkward. We fear a negative reaction to our expressions of how we feel. We are shy, or we think the other person already knows our feelings. There are endless excuses to keep our feelings to ourselves. **Communication** is not something we take time to practice, but the sooner we start building the habit, the better we will be.

Practice, especially protracted practice, does make perfect, as a study of Olympic athletes reveals. One difference between athletes who took home the gold and those who did not was that the top achievers started practicing their skills earlier in life. The implication is that the longer we practice something, the greater our chance of excelling at it – and that includes **Communication**.

Another critical aspect of skill development is applicable here – the principle of "overlearning." Learning something to a minimal level of proficiency does not help us retain that skill over long periods of time. To master something requires more practice than would seem necessary – in other words, overlearning a skill.

To apply effective **Communication** skills under pressure, a person needs to feel comfortable and natural with these skills. Proficiency comes from using these skills repeatedly. It is the same reason world-class musicians still begin practice sessions by playing the musical scales they learned as children – repeated practice creates a second-nature hand movement that is crucial for mastering the notes of challenging pieces.

The reward for practicing **Communication** skills is that you will feel better about yourself and your connections to the people around you. It also prepares you to face challenging circumstances with more confidence.

In my work as an executive coach, it is amazing how often my efforts are focused on helping a manager communicate with his or her staff, customers or peers. These are bright, talented, high-performing professionals who either resist expressing themselves or are unwilling to express themselves among colleagues in anything other than a calculated, logical or unemotional manner.

As a result, they lack the power of leadership that comes when the true leader makes an emotional connection with the follower and creates a bond that drives exceptional performance. These leaders genuinely believe that the workplace is no place for emotions, and, indeed, the thought of having to share what they "feel" is an extreme "fear factor" to many of them.

These **Communication** shut-ins try to tackle professional adversity with a minimum of emotional expenditure because they fear something they have not mastered. As a result, they try to motivate without sharing, to inspire without emotion, to build teams without building a connection. Inevitably they fail.

Why?

Because conquering adversity is all about heart. **Communication** – the art of sharing what we feel – gives our heart a voice. We call it passion, and no hero succeeds without it.

So how do we get started? How can we build a habit of **Communication** in our work?

Start with sharing what we already feel strongly about. Talk about the vision of the organization with your colleagues. Speak about the pride you have in your work and in your team. Share your passion for doing a job well. Tell people when they do

> **Communication** –
> the art of **sharing**
> what we **feel** – gives our
> **heart** a **voice**.
> We call it **passion**, and
> no **hero** succeeds without it.

something that you respect, admire or appreciate. Learn to verbalize positive thoughts as they occur.

Keep a box of thank-you cards in your desk, and write a quick note to someone who helped you finish a project on time, found information you needed, worked extra to cover the workload or did something else to help the team.

If you lead a team, keep a box of these notes available for team members to use in similar situations. If you don't want to write a note, then call people to thank them. Don't add any other business to your call; just express your appreciation and recognize their efforts.

STEP TWO

The second part of the **Communication Strategy** is to communicate now!

This aspect of **Communication** injects a sense of urgency to express what we feel. It is a reminder that the heart speaks loudest in the moment. Many times we "save" our emotions for "the right time" only to find when we get around to sharing how we feel that the impact has been lessened or that the opportunity never comes.

We must learn to communicate at the first opportunity when something strikes us as important. Consider this illustration:

> *I presented* Conquering Adversity *for the first time on August 10, 2001 – three years to the day after my wife and unborn son were killed. The presentation was made to twenty top executives of a communications company as a favor for a friend who had asked me to set aside the obvious trauma of the date and speak to this team of professionals.*

> *One hour into my seventy-five-minute keynote, the CEO stood up and left the room. He came back about five minutes later and stayed until I had finished. Afterward, every person thanked me for an unforgettable message. The CEO was the last to leave the room, and I made a point to apologize to him for what I interpreted as my having missed the mark with my message, given his sudden departure.*
>
> *"Quite the contrary," he replied. "I left to go back to my office. I closed my door, picked up the phone, called my wife, told her I loved her and that I would be home early tonight. I haven't done that in 25 years."*

We make a habit of missed opportunities to communicate with our colleagues. It isn't that we don't think about saying something to someone – passing on a compliment, congratulating a success, expressing our enjoyment at working with them. We just don't act on it.

Intentions become regrets when tomorrow doesn't come. We speak our minds about our jobs, so why don't we speak our hearts about the people? At that first presentation, it was the husband, not the CEO, who stood up and acted on the message he had heard.

What should you communicate today to someone in your life or at your work? Who is waiting to hear how you feel?

The actions required of this insight are relatively simple. They cost almost nothing, take virtually no time and yet are so uncommon to most of us.

You don't need to be a CEO to call your significant other and say you love him or her. It takes only courage to open your mouth and tell colleagues you are proud of something they did or that you appreciate working with them. Surprise your colleagues with coffee and donuts, invite someone from another department to have lunch, or send a thank-you card instead of an e-mail the next time someone does something to help you or your team.

The opportunities are in front of us every day to hone our **Communication** commitment. We just have to act on them. But skillful **Communication** saves us more than missed opportunities to speak from the heart. Communicating with a sense of urgency helps build strong teams at work, teams that produce bottom-line results for the organization.

Cultivating an environment in which team members feel empowered to openly share their opinions, feelings, reservations, pride and creativity accelerates the team-building process.

Communication brings people together. It builds trust, which is the foundation of any high-performing team. People need to know that their teammates respect who they are as much as what they bring to the team. Skill, expertise and experience are valuable assets on any team but no more so than trust, respect and passion. Passion is the catalyst for good chemistry in teams tackling tough problems with confidence and cohesiveness. Passion leads teams to meet deadlines and causes them to deliver the best solutions.

> **Communication**
> brings people
> **together**.

The difference between dysfunctional teams and high-impact

teams is rarely an absence of knowledge but more often an absence of chemistry – chemistry formulated by timely and sincere **Communication** among members.

STEP THREE

Finally, **invite others to help.**

Communicating what we feel is more than learning to express our appreciation, pride and other positive emotions. It is also about sharing how we accelerate success even in times of adversity.

In addition to letting people know that their presence is welcome, important and appreciated in our lives and in our workplaces, we also want them to understand how they can assist us in difficult times.

Communication removes assumptions, clarifies involvement and creates circumstances in which people know how to make a difference.

In my experience, inviting others to help after Cynthia's and Hunter's death accelerated our success in moving forward. In difficult times, people want to help but don't always know how. More important, they are reluctant to intrude.

My **Communication** with them cleared the way for their involvement. **Communication** is not always convenient, not always easy. Sometimes it asks a lot.

For months after Cynthia's death, there were many nights Ryan would cry for hours. He missed his mom. I tried to comfort him, hold him and reassure him, but often the tears just kept coming.

Many times, after holding him for several hours, I would

*find myself physically and emotionally drained. At that point,
I would reach out and call Jeannette, Ryan's godmother. I
knew all I had to say was, "I need help," and she would be
on her way.*

*No matter the hour, she would be there, curling up with
Ryan until he fell asleep and giving me just an hour or so
to close my eyes before all of us faced the next day. The
invitation to help was all Jeannette needed to be there when
it counted—but she could not know the need without my
willingness to communicate it.*

The lesson for our workplace is that **Communication** is effective
when it is candid, respected and welcome. Communicating is not
always easy or convenient. But when we speak with sincerity, our
message is heard.

We need to be able to reach out to our colleagues when the chips
are down and know that they will respond...and our colleagues
will help if they know help is needed and appreciated.

Communicating a sincere invitation for others to be involved
saves time, creates new solutions and instigates an urgency to
get results.

How often do we struggle with adversity in one area only to
find that someone in the next department or on another team or
just a phone call away had the answer that would have moved us
forward? Why doesn't that information get shared? Why do we not
reach out to others who can help? Again, we do what we practice,
or – more accurately – we don't do what we don't practice.

Communication breaks down barriers and brings people

together to achieving a common goal. It's good business sense as much as good common sense.

Communication gives our inner strength a powerful voice. It projects what we believe, what we expect and what we need in a way that builds people up, invites them into our lives, and rewards all of us with the ability to be more effective in the face of adversity.

STRATEGY #

1. Communicate with your heart.
2. Communicate now!
3. Invite others to help.

COMMUNICATION

Insight *Activity*

- ♦ Buy a box of thank-you cards and keep them out on your desk or on the kitchen counter at home so they are visible.

- ♦ Write at least two thank-you cards a week and mail or give them to friends, family, colleagues or neighbors. If there is something specific you want to acknowledge, then mention that. If not, just tell that person how much you appreciate him or her.

Insight *Activity*

- ♦ Complete the worksheet on the following page. It will be helpful to have a small bag (even a plastic sandwich bag) and a dozen marbles, stones, pennies, pieces of small candy, etc.

- ♦ Be honest in your responses and evaluate the results.

COMMUNICATE NOW!

Place a checkmark next to all of the statements that apply to you:

———— In the past week, I told a colleague that I appreciated working with him or her.

———— In the past week, I told a neighbor, friend or acquaintance "thank you" for something.

———— In the past week, I called a family member or friend for no reason other than to say, "I was thinking about you."

———— In the past week, I wrote a thank-you note for something someone did or for just being part of my life.

———— In the past week, I asked a friend to join me in a hobby that I do for fun or relaxation.

———— In the past week, I took a walk with someone just for the fun or exercise.

———— In the past week, my family ate dinner together at least four nights.

———— Each day in the past week, I told someone special that I love him or her.

———— In the past week, I told a colleague that I was proud of him or her.

———— In the past week, I volunteered my time at something important to me.

———— In the past week, I told my supervisor or other senior colleague that I appreciate his or her example, leadership or coaching.

———— In the past week, I called from work to tell someone he or she was special to me.

———— **Total number of checkmarks.**

Now, using a small bag and marbles, place one marble in the bag for each checkmark you made. Hold the bag up, look at it and visualize your Communications the past week. The more marbles in the bag, the more you took time to communicate. Is the bag as full as you would like? Have there been opportunities to communicate that were missed? Notice how easy it would be to have filled the bag. Consider how important it is to fill the bag every week. Communication is speaking with our hearts – in both a voice we hear and also in actions, invitations and time we share with others.

STRATEGY #

LOCOMOTION

"If you are going through hell, keep going."
~ Sir Winston Churchill ~

Steps in the **Locomotion** Strategy:

1. Create a "speed-is-life" mentality.

2. Adopt the mind-set of the traveler, not the settler.

3. Master the power of persistence.

"In the struggle between the stone and the water – in time, the water wins."

This Chinese proverb captures the essence of the **Locomotion** Strategy. There is enormous power in movement and nearly unstoppable power in persistent movement.

The Grand Canyon is one of the most stunning examples of

this truth – a picture of ageless beauty painted on a canvas of solid rock by the relentless force of rushing water. Wonderful things happen when we're in motion.

One of the greatest dangers in facing adversity, crisis or tragedy is that we panic, freeze and stop because we perceive the roadblocks, barriers or mountains in our life as insurmountable. To survive, we must push past that perception and adopt a philosophy of motion.

STEP ONE

The United States Air Force has known the **power of motion to overcome adversity for years.** Military flight schools teach young pilots a phrase "**speed-is-life**" – a phrase that comes with a corresponding action of pushing the aircraft's engine throttles forward to increase airspeed. The rationale is simple but very effective.

Speed-is-life teaches pilots to instinctively maximize airspeed when they encounter an in-flight emergency that threatens loss of control of the aircraft. Maximizing airspeed often allows the aircraft to respond better in a crisis. With maximum forward thrust, the aircraft handles better, and the pilot's margin for error in responding to the crisis increases with the throttles wide open.

Similarly, **Locomotion** is a technique that U.S. Special Forces use to overcome the disadvantage of being outnumbered by the enemy in an engagement.

These highly trained teams often find themselves in unplanned lethal situations in which the odds are significantly against their success or even their survival. **Locomotion** is the Strategy that evens the playing field.

Special Forces teams apply purposeful, coordinated motion where they are facing extreme adversity because it keeps the situation fluid and dynamic, puts their adversaries on the defensive and creates new opportunities for action that were not previously available.

The same principle is true in learning to move forward through our own life emergencies. People are able to respond better to crisis when they maximize their forward motion. Stagnation invites distress and amplifies adverse conditions.

> **Locomotion**
> **sharpens** our senses
> and creates
> **opportunities**
> for **success**...

Locomotion sharpens our senses and creates opportunities for success that might not otherwise be visible. When adversity threatens to overwhelm us, a speed-is-life instinct can even the playing field and keep us moving forward.

In the months and years after Cynthia's death, Ryan and I used travel as a means of keeping ourselves in motion, literally and emotionally.

He loved to travel, and setting travel plans for ourselves three or four times a year always kept something positive in front of us. During school breaks and summer vacations, we made trips with Cynthia's dad and mom, with her sister, with my mom, with my three brothers and their families, and sometimes on our own. Our plans gave us something to talk about, to look forward to, and they made new memories. Rarely were we idle.

Our travels were also adventures for a dad and his son. On one trip, Ryan and I surprised Cynthia's dad and mom by traveling to Mons, Belgium, to attend her father's retirement ceremony after more than 30 years of distinguished U.S. government service. On that occasion the two of us tackled bad weather, flight cancellations, rerouted connections and other travel woes but kept going. We arrived in time to attend the ceremony, and the impact was unmistakable.

That trip also created an opportunity for us to draw closer, to heal a bit more together and share some new smiles. We could have sent a card. We could have called to say congratulations, but by going there, we discovered a deeper sense of family.

That's what **Locomotion** does. By encouraging action, it creates a speed-is-life mentality that otherwise would not exist.

In the workplace, a speed-is-life mentality keeps our team, department or organization in motion, no matter what the obstacle. Locomotion teaches that imperfect action is preferable to perfect planning. The reason is that even imperfect action moves us in a direction, creating new opportunities that we might not have seen had we been stagnant.

> **Locomotion** teaches that imperfect **action** is preferable to perfect **planning**.

The perfect plan never accomplished anything without execution. When facing adversity, we must move in a determined, motivated manner, even if the outcome of our actions is not well defined.

Too often, our work teams bog down on one issue, one problem, one difficulty – and lose the overall project momentum. When that happens, we need to change direction, change focus and work on what we know, not lament what we don't.

It is critical to keep the team's energy, ideas and optimism flowing, even if the ultimate solution is still unclear—stay engaged and it will surface.

Step Two

The second step in **Locomotion** is the need to **adopt the mind-set of the traveler**, not the settler. We can condition ourselves to be change-ready rather than change-averse.

The traveler knows that change is the only constant. Every experience – enjoyable or challenging – is just a moment in time that will pass and bring new experience.

This is a critical perspective for overcoming adversity. The larger the calamity, the more likely we are to feel overwhelmed and paralyzed. The more serious the issue, the more it consumes us and the less agile we feel. But even a tragedy succumbs to time, provided we move forward with purpose and passion. **Locomotion** means keeping life moving, helping us believe that we can and will travel beyond the struggles of the moment.

In the workplace, having the mind-set of the traveler means that we can respond positively to change. It does not serve us well to become comfortable with today's reality because tomorrow the market, the competition, the product or the customer may encourage change or demand that we change today's norm.

The traveler's mind-set is ready to adapt to emerging opportunities, embrace unrealized potential and enjoy the newness of each experience.

The traveler's mind-set handles stress better than the settler because it is not locked into a territory, a location, a position or an opportunity.

Work to establish a mind-set that is change-agile, not change-averse. Work to develop a mind-set that is ready to go with the organization to new challenges rather than dig in on what used to be.

> **Embrace** the need to make **positive** things **happen.**

Adopting the traveler's mind-set also means embracing the need to make positive things happen, regardless of whether you like or agree with the changes you encounter. Hoping things will magically go back to the way they were will leave you disappointed, unproductive and frustrated. Life does not run backward, so it is best to move forward with it.

STEP THREE

The final step in the **Locomotion** Strategy is to **master the power of persistence.**

Calvin Coolidge was right when he said, "Nothing in the world can take the place of persistence." Developing a dogged spirit that refuses to yield is essential in unleashing our inner strength. **Winners never quit.** It is often their very refusal to capitulate that earns them this designation.

After Cynthia's death, there were many days I did not want to go to work because I was grieving my loss. No one would have denied me my retreat. No one would have criticized my pain, and no one would have begrudged me a day of abdicating my responsibilities. But the days I wanted to retreat were the days the son taught the father a lesson in the power of persistence.

I put Ryan on the bus for school each morning, and that picture fortified me when my strength waned. I remembered Ryan climbing on the bus each morning and turning to me with a smile and a wave. I remembered his face staring at me through the bus window as it pulled away – a face that carried both pain and hope as he searched to see if I was still waving, as if that reassured him that today would be alright.

His loss was as great as mine, his burden heavier, and yet he persisted. If Ryan could get on that bus each morning, carrying this burden at nine years old, then I could drive to the office and be a professional.

The power of persistence isn't something you learn as you age. It's something you master as you mature – a lesson taught to me by a hero so young.

"There is nothing more important than persistence in success," Paul Martin says. "Everything I've persevered at, I've achieved."

Martin ought to know a lot about persistence and achievement. In 1999, he finished in 153rd place in the grueling Hawaiian Ironman triathlon, finishing ahead of 1,200 other athletes who had a significant advantage over Martin. They had both legs. Martin is an amputee who competed with a prosthetic leg.

Are you a Paul Martin? Do you have the internal fortitude to accept what you cannot change and still push yourself to achieve?

We can be role models for persistence every day in our workplace. How we apply ourselves often speaks louder than our final result. Finishing 153rd in a race would be considered failure in some business mentalities, but not if the effort was extraordinary and not if the result was 1,200 places better than more able competitors.

Mastering the power of persistence means we come to work every day because our organization needs our talents, energy and ideas. We set aside petty excuses and fulfill our commitment to our team. We respect our team members by being there – fully present – for our jobs.

The power of persistence says that overcoming adversity is exhausting, frustrating work, but it is not more than we can manage. It is not stronger than our most determined efforts. Our progress may be slow, even imperceptible at times, but we know it is there because we continue to push back on the adversity we face.

Moving forward means never relinquishing the will to win, regardless of the place you finish. That is the essence of a hero's strength – heroes refuse to surrender and therefore cannot be defeated.

STRATEGY #

1. Create a "speed-is-life" mentality.

2. Adopt the mind-set of the traveler, not the settler.

3. Master the power of persistence.

LOCOMOTION

Insight *Activity*

Steps to the Summit

Locomotion is a Strategy that reminds us to keep moving in the direction of our life priorities. There is tremendous power in motion, particularly when it is focused and purposeful.

Progress toward life priorities is not so much a distance covered as it is an effort expended—the highest summits in the world are reached by climbers who take steps measuring no more than a few inches at a time. They just keep taking them.

What are three (3) goals in your life that you have not yet achieved?

1. _____

2. _____

3. _____

Where are three (3) places in the world you have not yet visited but would like to?

1. _____

2. _____

3. _____

Who would you like to spend more quality time with?

How will you keep your dreams and goals visible in your life?

What is one action you can take now to move forward on one of the insights you just wrote?

STRATEGY # 5

COLLABORATION

---

*"The friend in my adversity I shall always cherish most.
I can better trust those who helped to relieve the gloom
of my dark hours than those who are so ready
to enjoy with me the sunshine of my prosperity."*

~ Ulysses S. Grant ~

Steps in the **Collaboration** Strategy:

1. Create a Collaboration Circle.

2. Welcome empathy, not sympathy.

3. Seek balance.

With Ryan set to enter fourth grade less than one month after Cynthia's death, one of my main concerns was selecting a teacher who had the compassion and patience to deal with what certainly would be an ongoing struggle for this nine-year-old.

For obvious reasons, the school district had a policy

prohibiting parents from requesting or selecting teachers, but in this instance Driver Middle School's principal, Mr. Pat Collier, made an exception, given the severity of the trauma and a desire to do what was in Ryan's best interest. He and I discussed the kind of teacher who would be the best fit for this unique situation. His recommendation was a young, creative and very student-centered teacher who seemed ideal for the challenge. Her name should also have been a sign – Ms. Suzanne Novak.

Though not related to our family, the stunning coincidence in last names left us wondering if even that would be too much for Ryan in his fragile state. But any concerns were quickly cast aside as Suzanne Novak became a linchpin in guiding Ryan back to a sense of normalcy and focus. She was unbelievable!

There were instances when Ryan would break down in class, sometimes without warning. It might have been someone talking about their mom or something in a book they were reading or a holiday or any of the endless reasons grief creeps from our hearts to our faces. Whatever the reason, Ms. Novak had a beanbag chair at the back of the class, behind a low partition. It was a reading area but also doubled as Ryan's space.

When the tears came, he could leave his desk, go back to the beanbag chair and use whatever time he needed to gather himself together, rejoining the class when he was ready. On occasion, she even took him into a quiet hallway, sat on the floor, and held him until the pain passed. Remarkably, never once did a single child in his class laugh at him, tease him or do anything but care about him. They were, and are, his friends, and they knew he was hurting.

As his teacher, Ms. Novak made Ryan do his fourth-

grade work just like every other child in class, but she also realized that he was different. Ms. Novak knew Ryan went to war – emotional war – each day, and she was impressed with how valiantly he fought. She often told me she was "privileged" to know Ryan, but it was Ryan and I who were privileged to have her in our lives.

The **Collaboration** Strategy is all about that kind of humanity. It's about a principal who knows it is more important to bend a rule than break a child. It's about children with the capacity to care about a classmate and friend, and it is most certainly about a teacher with the heart to reach out to a grieving little boy and make a real difference in his life.

Collaboration is about the people we take with us on our journey forward. It is about those we choose and those who choose us, about those we know and many we don't. It is about people who step forward and say, "I'm here to help."

Arguably, **Collaboration** is the most important Strategy because, quite often, the challenge we face is not one we can overcome alone. Nor should we attempt to meet adversity with no one to support us. Here's the critical aspect – this Strategy must be developed before a crisis arises, not afterward. Trying to forge a trusted circle of support in the midst of crisis is almost impossible. **Collaboration** means cultivating positive, supportive relationships when times are

> **Collaboration** is about the **people** we take with us on our **journey** forward.

not challenging so that when they become difficult, the network is already in place to help.

STEP ONE

Collaboration brings a team that can conquer adversity, and teams are built on relationships.

By definition, **Collaboration** is the act of working with one or more individuals on something. One cannot collaborate with oneself. **Collaboration** asks the questions, "Whom am I taking with me on this journey? Whom do I trust? Who is there for me, especially when the bottom falls out? Who wants to help? Who is able to help?"

These are not trivial questions. They invite consideration of three important factors – trust, compatibility and availability.

"Trust" means that you surround yourself with people who have demonstrated that they have your best interests at heart and respect your confidence.

The second factor, compatibility, is the measure of a good listener and an energizing presence. It is critical to have people around you who can be a sounding board, a strong shoulder or a positive influence.

The third factor, availability, means people are accessible and willing to give you their time, either in person or on the phone. Having people to connect with is essential for countering the inevitable feelings of isolation and anxiety that accompany extreme adversity.

Discovering our inner hero also means discovering those who

make us stronger – or what I call our "**Collaboration** Circle."

A **Collaboration** Circle is the support network we develop. Think of it in terms of a bull's eye with you at the center and a series of concentric rings moving out from the center. The closer the ring is to the center, the stronger the connection to you and the

> **Discovering** our inner **hero** also means discovering those who make us **stronger.**

more likely the person is to partner with you in your efforts to move forward. If you're having trouble deciding what ring people would fit best in, then use the "snowstorm" exercise.

You are driving at night on a back-country road in a raging blizzard when your car slides into a ditch. You are unhurt. There are no other cars on the road, and it is unlikely that any will come along. You have a cell phone with barely enough battery to make one call. The people you put in the inner circle – the ring closest to the bull's eye – are those who would immediately come find you, no matter what the weather.

The people in the Support Team ring – the next ring out – would wait for a break in the weather and then come get you. The people in the Bullpen ring would notify the police that you were stranded and ask them to rescue you.

All of these people care about you, but their actions are different, based on their perceived connection to you.

There is a **Collaboration** Circle activity at the end of this chapter to help you visualize your own network.

Teams, either informal or formal, are the backbone of most organizations. We have project teams, leadership teams, sales teams, marketing teams, human resources teams, engineering teams, production teams, customer service teams, finance teams, creative teams, training teams, executive teams, frontline teams and every other kind of team imaginable. The one commonality in every single team is people, and that means relationship dynamics.

Collaboration is about the strength of those teams and the actions we can take to make them unstoppable.

What teams are you on? How close are you to the people you work with? How well do you know them or try to know them? How many names would fill the inner ring of your **Collaboration Circle** at work? Who stands with you, no matter the difficulty?

Take stock of the support network you have in your organization, because success on the job, including your own success, is built on the strength of professional relationships – not organizational charts.

It is critical to develop sincere professional relationships with our colleagues because that is the foundation of trust, and trust is the one commodity we cannot manufacture, conjure or buy. Trust has to be earned face-to-face.

Use team meetings to do more than cover an operational agenda. Use them to promote esprit de corps, build morale and develop professional relationships. Leaders should include a team-building activity at least once a month, delegating responsibility for that activity to meeting attendees, but insisting on its priority. Followers should ask for more team-oriented training or involvement, bringing ideas forward to their supervisors and volunteering to take a leadership role in facilitating the activities.

The time to build a team is before adversity strikes. You cannot build a shelter in a hurricane.

STEP TWO

Collaboration welcomes empathy, not sympathy.

The people spilled out of the funeral home, onto the porch and up the sidewalk in an unbroken line stretching farther than I could see. There were hundreds waiting quietly, patiently to pay their respects during the visitation.

People came who loved Cynthia like a sister, and people came who had never met her. Colleagues from Syracuse China Company came by the dozens – management and production – people who were close to me and people who had battled me on nearly every work issue. People I had fired came and waited in line. Co-workers came from the hospital where Cynthia worked. Neighbors came. Friends came.

The next day, the church was filled for the funeral. Relatives I had not seen in decades drove hundreds of miles through the night or flew in to be there for Ryan and me.

One cousin and his family arrived from Cleveland early that morning. Driving into the village of Marcellus, they asked a woman in our neighborhood where they might get a bite of breakfast before the funeral. The woman replied that we did not have a restaurant open at that hour but told them to pull into her driveway and she would fix them all something to eat. I had never met the woman.

Family and friends from out of town stayed in the homes of people in our neighborhood who volunteered to take people in. People away on vacation called to tell us where their house keys were and opened their doors to anyone who needed a room. For almost six months, neighbors and friends delivered dinner nearly every night to our back porch – hot, fresh, homemade and delicious. I still have pans that belong to them.

No one made people do these things. No one even asked. They just did.

Empathy is caring in action. Sympathy is caring from a distance. Empathy is a connection with people that draws you closer. Sympathy cares but doesn't act. Empathy stands in line for hours, drives or flies hundreds of miles, cooks breakfast for a stranger, opens their homes, makes dinners for months, and more. Empathy, as part of the **Collaboration** Strategy, is more than reaching out to feel what the other person is experiencing. It is sharing that experience with the person to whatever extent is possible. When the challenge is to conquer extreme adversity, winners welcome empathy, not sympathy.

> **Empathy** is **caring** in **action.**

Practicing empathy at work starts with going the extra mile for the organization and your colleagues. It means doing more than what is expected, more than what is asked—and doing it willingly.

Empathy understands that conquering adversity on the job means we need to do more than care about colleagues. We need to become part of the solution. How can we help? Who can we ask?

What can we bring to the table?

Saying 'that's too bad" or "sorry that happened" when the going gets tough for another person, another team or the organization is not applying the empathy aspect of **Collaboration**. Don't wait for someone to tell you what you already know can be helpful. Do it. Take responsibility for acting on a need. Let your actions speak louder than your words.

On teams, empathy also means applying the Steven Covey principle of "seek first to understand, then to be understood." It means listening first to other team members, hearing their points of view well enough to explain them, and telling colleagues that you want to understand their ideas, input and insight because together you may find an even better solution.

Empathy gives the benefit of the doubt when a decision seems questionable but you respect the source. It is proactive in its efforts to reach out, understand and be involved. Organizations excel when their associates don't hesitate to practice empathy.

STEP THREE

The third step in the **Collaboration** strategy is balance. **We must always seek balance between work and family.**

Work-life balance is not an either-or proposition. Both are necessary; both add value, but balance is the difference between living to work and working to live. Too many of us sacrifice the quality of our personal lives on the altar of professional success. We justify spending extra hours at work by thinking it will help our families in the long run. Realistically, it helps no one.

Organizations and colleagues do not benefit from team members who are tired, unfocused and frustrated. Families and friends do not benefit from our absence, regardless of our motives. In the end, we do both work and life an injustice when we fail to balance the two. Sure, it's important to be productive and effective in your organization. It is admirable to be dedicated to excellence in your work and to inspire your colleagues to do the same. Leaders and followers alike should work with pride and give their very best every day, but seeking balance does not mean slacking off. Quite the contrary – it means bringing your A-game to every situation, personal or professional.

Research confirms that work-life balance is as much a business issue as it is a personal issue. Organizations that support work-life balance have achieved:

♦ Increased productivity

♦ Improved recruitment and retention

♦ Lower rates of absenteeism

♦ An improved customer experience

♦ A more motivated workforce

These are win-win results for both employer and employee. But whether at work or at home, balance requires us to be fully present.

One of the biggest mistakes we make is to be physically in one location but mentally in another. We are not at our best in either circumstance. Being fully present means that we are completely engaged in the moment, giving our full attention and effort.

Today's best organizations know, even with escalating professional demands, that working is still a poor substitute for living. People

need to have lives outside work in order to enjoy their lives at work.
Leaders in companies that value work-life balance know people
need to work as hard at being a good parent or partner or volunteer
as they do at being a good manager, teacher or assistant.

High-performing organizations encourage team members to
pursue interests and passions in their personal lives because that
energy comes back to the organization in high morale and high
retention rates.

Visionary organizations share the pride their employees experience
when attending their child's school event because they know that
people who are happy outside work bring that satisfaction with
them to the workplace.

We must seek balance.

I am a proud professional who sets
high standards and believes in making a
difference in whatever workplace I engage.
I pour passion and energy into whatever I

We **must**
seek **balance.**

do and take my obligations seriously. However, if life experience
has taught me anything, it is that we must value life if we are to
make work-life balance a reality.

I believe the most important titles in life are found on greeting
cards – not business cards. These are the titles that say "Dad,"
"Mom," "Wife," "Husband," "Partner," "Friend" or "To
Someone Special."

We must seek balance, always balance.

STRATEGY #

1. Create a Collaboration Circle.
2. Welcome empathy, not sympathy.
3. Seek balance.

COLLABORATION

Insight *Activity*

♦ On the following page, complete your own Collaboration Circle. Write down the names of people in your life based on how close they are to you and how readily they support you.

MY COLLABORATION CIRCLE

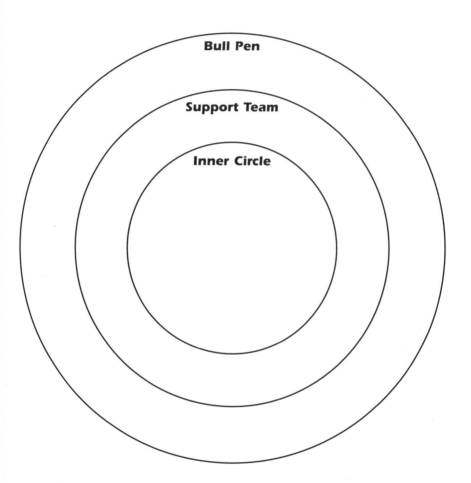

Write down the names of people in your life based on how closely connected they are to you. Then examine your results…what kind of support network do you have? What circles need developing?

STRATEGY #6

CELEBRATION

---

*"Happiness...is not a destination: it is a manner of traveling.
Happiness is not an end in itself. It is a by-product
of working, playing, loving and living."*

~ Haim Ginott ~

Steps in the **Celebration** Strategy:

1. Experience laughter.

2. Schedule downtime.

3. Create positive consequences
   from negative events.

*"...under extreme pressure, **the ability to lighten up, celebrate
and laugh can make all the difference.** It can break a spiral of
depression and stimulate creativity. It can enable people to step back
and get psychological distance on their problem. It can cut through
fear and tension."*

Dennis Perkins' observation in his book *Leading at the Edge* captured the essence of one secret to Ernest Shackleton's heroic efforts in leading 28 men in 1914 on a two-year Antarctic survival saga. As they faced extreme adversity, their ability to laugh and celebrate made a critical difference. How?

It may seem out of place to talk about **Celebration** as a Strategy for moving forward with purpose and passion, but for those who have experienced extreme hardship, the connection is obvious.

> **Celebration** feeds our **positive energy** and our **sense of hope.**

Celebration feeds our positive energy and our sense of hope. It nourishes our spirits, refreshes our attitudes and gives us strength to fight off the inevitable attacks of negativism and fear that accompany severe adversity.

STEP ONE

Celebration is not ignorance of the seriousness of a situation but a recognition that, despite the harshness of the circumstance, there must be room in the human experience to laugh – if only to break the sense of fear and anxiety.

It is easy to sink.

Consider a drowning sailor. It takes no energy at all to succumb to the sea and sink beneath the waves. The hard part is staying alive, staying afloat, fighting for every breath, kicking and paddling for some distant, even unseen, shoreline. **Celebration** rescues us from the exhaustion of fighting the good fight. It renews our energy, lifts our spirits and keeps us afloat.

There are just some people who know how to use **Celebration** *better than others. Ken Fish is one of those people and one of my best friends.*

In the years since Cynthia's death, Ken has made it his mission to create opportunities, both large and small, for **Celebration** *to work its magic in our journey forward. He hosts summer barbeques, organizes neighborhood gatherings and invites us to dinner, the theater or sporting events.*

He is selfless in his commitment to infusing each day with a sense of "what went right." Ken is the first to laugh at himself or get together on a whim, and he constantly reminds me in his actions and attitude about the power of **Celebration** *to rejuvenate the spirit.*

Celebration *is not about forgetting anything but about remembering everything, including the zest, joy, smiles and laughs that were so much a part of our lives with Cynthia.*

In our workplace, **Celebration** is too often absent. You can change that. Think of the impact on morale at work if you started a "What Went Right?" bulletin board and allowed people to post a note celebrating some small victory in their personal or professional lives.

Imagine a supervisor whose cover memo on a meeting agenda has a tasteful but humorous cartoon or a witty quote that tickles the mind and brings a chuckle.

Celebration is never at someone else's expense, and respect always needs to govern our actions, but a workplace where people take work seriously and themselves lightly is a more productive, motivated and successful environment.

Missed the quarterly numbers? Production counts below expectations? Customer complaints? What impact would using a sports bloopers video to open a team meeting have on a tense, anxious group expecting their leader to drop the hammer?

It would set the tone that even superstars drop the ball once in a while. It would lighten the air with the realization that great teams recover from mistakes. The meeting focus will still be serious, but the tension would be reduced and the receptiveness of the participants increased – a win for the organization and its people.

In our own professional workday, humorous moments offer us an opportunity to refresh our spirit and the spirits of our co-workers – if we are not afraid to be the first to laugh at ourselves.

STEP TWO

Celebration also gives our support team some much-needed downtime.

Recalling that conquering adversity is a team effort reminds us that there are those close to us who also need to relax their focus and release some of their anxieties. **Celebration** is powerful emotional medicine for everyone engaged in the adversity battle. I learned this lesson less than one month after Cynthia's death.

My birthday was less than one month after Cynthia died and was the first family holiday Ryan and I encountered. I had told Ryan not to do anything special for my birthday, as both of us, I thought, just needed to skip the day.

That year our friends and neighbors taught us about Celebration as a Strategy to move forward. A few days before my birthday, Jeannette took Ryan shopping after school and wrapped a couple of presents with him while Ken and other neighbors pitched in to make a cake, decorate a bit and add a few presents of their own. When I arrived home from work, a small party had already started in my backyard. Together, we shared cake and ice cream, opened presents, laughed about ordinary things, and watched Ryan and some of the neighbor children play. It was a wonderful evening, full of smiles and laughs among people who also were grieving the loss we all shared.

It was important for us to overlay sad memories with happier ones. That year, laughing and celebrating with our friends not only made Ryan and me feel good, but it also made our friends feel good. Everyone got a boost. These happy times cushioned the pain we all felt. The more smiles we put between our lives and our tears, the more we would all move forward.

Celebration would not erase the tragedy, but it would help us all gather the strength necessary to overcome our loss.

Research shows that children laugh an average of 200 times a day, adults barely 17 times. We can learn much from children's ability to laugh, especially in the workplace. A childlike sense of **Celebration** can help maximize what people are capable of accomplishing.

Whether it is an informal gathering around the water cooler to recognize a team member or a formal event to rally the troops, the act of getting together, smiling, laughing and sharing stories is priceless for a group that has worked hard to overcome adversity.

On a more personal level, taking a colleague aside to share a cup of coffee, a lunch or a surprise visit when you know that person has struggled with something recently is a win-win random act of kindness.

STEP THREE

Celebration also means **creating positive consequences from negative events.**

For example, at the university where Cynthia graduated with a bachelor's degree in cytotechnology, I endowed a scholarship in her name. Each spring, Upstate Medical University in Syracuse selects one cytotechnology student to receive the Cynthia A. Novak Memorial Scholarship, a scholarship celebrating her life while helping others with their education.

Cynthia also enjoyed the zoo. Animals were a passion of hers, and snow leopards were her favorite. It was natural, then, for Ryan and me to buy a memorial bench at the zoo we had so often visited together and to place it in front of the snow leopard exhibit. There it provides people with a chance to sit and rest, and it is our first stop each time we visit the zoo. The plaque reads, "In memory of Cynthia Novak, whose love embraced all creatures."

But creating positive results from negative events doesn't have to involve donations, recognition or money. The closeness of my relationship with Ryan is one of the most positive outcomes we have created. We are as close as any father and son can be, and it warms my heart every night when we say goodnight, tap foreheads and never fail to say "I love you."

The strength and depth of my friendships have also increased. I value positive people in my life and make an effort to express that appreciation. My perspective on life has also changed for the better as I have found an inner peace that allows me to love both what I had and what I have – to count blessings, not tears.

Creating positive outcomes from negative events carries a powerful message in the workplace as well. Organizations that grapple with downsizings, layoffs, re-engineering, reorganization or other internal upheavals need ways for people to reconnect, bond and see the change for what it is, a necessary alignment.

Creating **positive** outcomes from negative events carries a **powerful** message.

At times like this, organizations can increase their involvement in the community, in charities or in education as a way to refocus people in a positive direction. Organizing associates to volunteer at a local school's reading hour, a food bank, a cancer-awareness run or similar activities strengthens working relationships, draws colleagues closer to old acquaintances and encourages making new ones. Charitable work as a group is a great way to reinforce the fact that, even with ongoing business challenges, there are always those climbing steeper summits.

Amid adversity, there are still ways to lift morale, productivity and optimism by knowing that positive outcomes are easier to see with our heads up.

Perhaps the most surprising positive consequence for me after

Cynthia's death was discovering the strength I had inside. It was my personal struggle that freed that strength and showed me what life is truly about. The gift of living the Six Strategies has created an inner confidence, a personal peace and a passion for life that has changed me forever.

I hope in sharing my message that it changes you as well.

We must celebrate life, cherish love and choose happiness. We are not masters of the seas and cannot direct the winds, but we sail our own ships, chart our own course and have the power to choose. Never give away that power. Do not let it be taken away, and never let it waste away. For all its imperfections, injustices and wrongs, life is still a beautiful gift.

There is a strength inside each of us just waiting to be discovered. You are stronger than you know, more resilient than you realize, more capable than you can imagine. But it need not take adversity to find that strength – you can find it today. You can unleash this strength in your personal and professional lives – the Strategy is to believe that your strength has been there all along.

STRATEGY #6

1. Experience laughter.

2. Schedule downtime.

3. Create positive consequences from negative events.

CELEBRATION

TODAY

Today, my life – both professionally and personally – is full, blessed and successful. Ryan is a high honor roll student, plays first chair alto saxophone in the high school band and is a three-sport athlete. He volunteers in our church and is an exceptional brother. As a young man with a bright future, he is a remarkable example of how we can overcome even the greatest adversity – and he has taught me more about living life than I will ever teach him. We are as close as father and son can get and together have a new life that honors our past.

I remarried in 2001. My wife, Jeannette, is an angel without wings. She is Ryan's godmother – the woman Cynthia chose to raise Ryan if she were ever not there – and the person who, after me, has most influenced Ryan's recovery. She has been part of Ryan's life since the day he was born. At his baptism, as Jeannette held Ryan in her arms for the blessing, Cynthia leaned over to me and whispered, "If anything ever happens to me, that is who I want raising my son." Her wish is now our life.

Jeannette is my friend, strength and love, and I believe she was placed in our lives to show us that life goes on. In 2003, we welcomed Connor James to our family. He is a precious reminder that love is eternal.

Professionally, I found success as director of human resources for Cornell University and later as a consultant, writer and speaker. Whether I am training groups of managers, coaching senior executives, facilitating team-building activities at conferences, or giving motivational keynotes, the principles of *Conquering Adversity* and the *Six Strategies* message are an integral part of my work.

Special people abound in my life. My mother, my three brothers, my best friend, Cynthia's parents and sister, close colleagues, and neighbors all add to the richness of each day. My **Collaboration** circle is deep with people who make a difference in our lives.

TALE OF TWO JARS

When surfing the Web some time back, I came across one of those crazy invitations from a healthy living website to calculate how long I would live. I clicked on the site and quickly answered a series of health-related questions. Finished, I waited for the big answer…77 years.

Having just celebrated my 42nd birthday, I was struck by the fact that just 35 years separated the life I knew today from the hereafter. It was sobering – not a lot of time, really, especially considering all that I want to do with my life and with those I love.

But working through that calculator made me realize that time is one resource we all have too little of and that how we spend our time is so important. I wondered how well I was using my time. Was I making the most of it? I wondered how I could remind myself every day that time is both fleeting and precious.

The answer came in two jars. Odd as it may seem, these two jars have helped me keep focus not only on appreciating the time I have but also on making the most of it.

In my office, I keep two large, clear glass jars. I filled one of the jars with 1,820 clear glass stones, the kind you find at a hobby shop for use in flower arrangements and decorations. The 1,820 stones represent the number of weeks between my 42nd birthday and my hypothetical date with destiny at age 77. This jar holds the time that I have left. Each Monday, I take one stone out and discard it to represent the week of my life that has just passed. Thus each week this jar holds fewer stones. The act of removing a stone and the knowledge that the jar holds fewer and fewer "weeks" give me a powerful visual reminder that my time on this planet is finite and passing.

The second jar holds a different collection of glass stones. These are multicolored, and while their number is still far fewer than the 1,820 that I started with in the other jar, they are even more precious. This is my "Live, Love, Balance" jar.

Each time that I do something special with my family or with friends or for myself, I place a colored stone in this jar. Each time that I volunteer my time for something I believe in, I place a colored stone in the jar. Each time that I enrich my own spiritual, emotional, physical or intellectual health, I add a colored stone to the jar.

Each time that I make time for my children, my spouse, my friends, my neighbors or my community in an activity that brings us closer or creates a shared experience, I add another stone to the jar. It could be helping one son with his homework, taking a walk with my wife, taking the family to the zoo, watching a movie together on Friday night, sharing dinner with friends, or any of countless other experiences that place love, friendship, family or fun ahead of professional demands.

The different colors remind me that there are an infinite number of ways to add value to the time we have, while the growing number of colored stones in this jar gives me a visual barometer of how effectively I am balancing my work and personal life. I want this jar to overflow someday – I want to see it grow daily, weekly, monthly, yearly, so I work harder at finding ways to "earn" another colored stone.

This jar helps me push away from my desk and toss the football with my son. It helps me leave the office early to make a school band concert or to plan a weekend getaway with the family rather than flying in early to a business meeting.

There is also a satisfaction in knowing that beautiful things are happening in my life in the time that I am given – and while I may not remember what special event each of those colored stones represents, I do know that it was special.

Yes, the clear stones diminish each week, regardless of whether I have spent the time wisely or wasted it—but the colored stones tell the more important story, for as that jar overflows, so does the joy, happiness and peace in my life.

It is impossible to express how much I miss Cynthia and Hunter. It is a pain that is never quelled, but I have learned to count blessings, not tears, and my life is richly blessed.

My desire, as you work through any adversity, large or small, is that sharing my experience will help you discover your own strength – the strength to overcome…and to win…that resides within all of us.

"Nuggets" of Wisdom from the Six Strategies

Affirmation

♦ "Most of us spend more time each week deciding what food to put into our carts at the grocery store than we spend understanding what values we put into our lives."

♦ "Values that are visible are viable."

♦ "It is the sum of kept promises, even small ones, that builds our credibility and effectiveness with colleagues."

♦ "Fear is the power that adversity holds over us, and the more we dwell on our fear, the more power we give it."

♦ "Affirmation teaches us to become emotional archeologists, searching the ruins of our situation for remnants of what is still valuable, relevant and important."

Expectation

♦ "Expectation refocuses the vision and takes us beyond today with a forward-thinking perspective. It does not ignore today's reality but it does not become mired in it, either."

♦ "As leaders, team members, or individual contributors, we must adjust our Expectations to accept the truth that life – and work – are not always fair and that even in this reality, we must excel."

♦ "The unchallenged fact is that we need more optimism on the job. We need people who think like winners, talk like winners and act like winners. Our organizations will thrive when our people can 'see' tomorrow as better than today because they are making it better."

♦ "It is impossible to drive a car by looking into the rear view mirror to see where we have been. Our priority is to see where we are going. In the same way, tackling adversity means moving forward with the knowledge that some questions need action, not answers."

Communication

♦ "Communication is not about talking. It's about sharing."

♦ "Conquering adversity is all about heart. Communication – the art of sharing what we feel – gives our heart a voice. We call it passion and no hero succeeds without it."

♦ "We do what we practice – or more accurately – we don't do what we don't practice."

♦ "The difference between dysfunctional teams and high-impact teams is rarely an absence of knowledge but more often an absence of chemistry – chemistry formulated by timely and sincere Communication among members."

♦ "Communication is effective when it is candid, respected and welcome. Communicating is not always easy or convenient. But when we speak with sincerity, our message is heard."

Locomotion

♦ "In the struggle between the stone and the water – in time, the water wins."

♦ "The traveler knows that change is the only constant. Every experience – enjoyable or challenging – is just a moment in time that will pass and bring new experience."

♦ "People are able to respond better to crisis when they maximize their forward motion. Stagnation invites distress and amplifies adverse conditions. Locomotion sharpens our senses and creates opportunities for success that might not otherwise be visible."

♦ "The perfect plan never accomplished anything without execution. When facing adversity, we must move in a determined, motivated manner, even if the outcome of our actions is not well defined."

♦ "The power of persistence says that overcoming adversity is exhausting, frustrating work, but it is not more than we can manage. It is not stronger than our most determined efforts."

Collaboration

♦ "Collaboration is about the people we take with us on our journey forward. It is about those we choose and those who choose us, about those we know and many we don't. It is about people who step forward and say, "I'm here to help."

♦ "The time to build a team is before adversity strikes. You cannot build a shelter in a hurricane."

♦ "Practicing empathy at work starts with going the extra mile for the organization and your colleagues. It means doing more than what is expected, more than what is asked – and doing it willingly."

♦ "Today's best organizations know, even with escalating professional demands, that working is still a poor substitute for living. People need to have lives outside work in order to enjoy their lives at work.

Celebration

♦ "Celebration rescues us from the exhaustion of fighting the good fight. It renews our energy, lifts our spirits, and keeps us afloat."

♦ "Amid adversity, there are still ways to lift morale, productivity, and optimism by knowing that positive outcomes are easier to see with our head up."

♦ "You are stronger than you know, more resilient than you realize, more capable than you can imagine."

♦ "We must celebrate life. We are not masters of the seas and cannot direct the winds but we sail our own ships, chart our own course and have the power to choose. Never give away that power. Do not let it be taken away and never let it waste away. For all its imperfections, injustices and wrongs, life is still a beautiful gift."

The Author

Christopher Novak started The Summit Team
(www.**summit-team**.com) as an extension of
over 20 years of professional experience in
positions that included Director of Human
Resources for Cornell University's Campus
Life division, Human Resources Manager for

Syracuse China Company, a unit of Libbey Inc., and as an officer
and military aviator. An experienced human resources executive, his
expertise includes training design and facilitation, employee relations,
recruitment, coaching, and leadership. His passionate stage presence
and genuine rapport, make him a sought after performance coach,
skills trainer, and motivational speaker.

He has authored more than 20 articles for magazines that include
*Newsweek, HR Magazine, Human Resource Professional, Air & Space,
Retired Officer* and *The New York Times Syndicate*. Novak has a
master's degree in business management, specializing in human
resources, from the State University of New York's College of
Technology and a dual bachelor's degree in aeronautics-
mathematics from Miami University (Ohio).

Bring Christopher Novak and the powerful message of

***Conquering Adversity: Six Strategies to Move You and
Your Team Through Tough Times***

to your next conference, special event,
leadership development outing, or team meeting.

Keynotes and workshops available.

Contact   The Summit Team
by email: conqueringadversity@summit-team.com
by U.S. mail: 16 E. Main Street, Suite 200, Marcellus, NY 13108
or by phone: 315.673.1323

Additional CornerStone Leadership Resources:

The Ant and the Elephant is a different kind of book for a different kind of leader! A great story that teaches that we must lead ourselves before we can expect to be an effective leader of others. **$12.95**

Start Right – Stay Right is every employee's straight-talk guide to personal responsibility and job success. Perfect for every employee at every level, from seasoned co-workers to new staff additions. **$9.95**

Too Many Emails contains dozens of tips and techniques to increase your email effectiveness and efficiency. **$9.95**

175 Ways to Get More Done in Less Time has 175 really good suggestions that will help you get things done faster...usually better. **$9.95**

Becoming the Obvious Choice is a roadmap showing employees how they can maintain their motivation, develop their hidden talents, and become the best. **$9.95**

Leadership ER is a powerful story that shares valuable insights on how to achieve and maintain personal health, business health and the critical balance between the two. Read it and develop your own prescription for personal and professional health and vitality. **$14.95**

Goal Setting for Results addresses the fundamentals of setting and achieving your goal of moving yourself and your organization from where you are, to where you want (and need) to be! **$9.95**

136 Effective Presentation Tips is a powerful handbook providing 136 practical, easy-to-use tips to make every presentation a success. **$9.95**

You Gotta Get In The Game...Playing to Win in Business, Sports and Life provides direction on how to get into and win the game of life and business. **$14.95**

Ethics 4 Everyone is a real-world guide for corporate leaders on how to lead with integrity. Following these guidelines will help your company win the right way. **$9.95**

Visit www.**cornerstoneleadership**.com
for additional books and resources.